a lump of sugar
and
a dash of spice

poems by wauneta hackleman

Northwoods Press, Inc.

Library of Congress Catalog Card Number: 80-80782.

ISBN 0-89002-147-3, Paperback
ISBN 0-89002-148-1, Cloth

Northwoods Press
PO Box 249
Stafford, VA 22554

Cover Art: Elizabeth Bentley

Some of these poems have been published in
*Cycloflame, Voices International, Poet,
Pancontinental Anthology, Sandcutters*. Some
are prize winning poems.

Other books by the author:

HOW TO SLAY A DRAGON

SOLILOQUIES IN VERSE

Dedicated to all the strangers
in airports and in the crowds
who have, unknowingly, supplied
me with the ideas for many of
the poems in this book

and to

my son

STEPHEN

To Mary
whose life touched
mine.

        Wanneta

May some poem
walk with you
through a memory.

It is as necessary to love as to breathe.
There is no life without either.

—Author

Alas! The love of women! It is known to be
a fearful thing; for all of theirs upon that
die is thrown; and if it is lost, life has no
more to bring to them but mockeries of the
past alone.

—Byron

MY SONG IS UNSUNG

We were like the first eight bars
of the Impossible Dream
staccotoed with want
and meaning to make it happen
but it didn't.
Like an unfinished painting
in the attic
we covered our secrets
not speaking the truth
our eyes did it for us.
Time was not on our side.
I left you at the airport
with my song unsung.
You will find the sheet music
on your piano bench.

FLIGHT 425

The travel agent
on the fifth floor
insisted I take
the trip to Barbados
B W I A Flight #425.

He talked of white beaches
        coconut palms
                cuisines
                        plush hotels.

Odd.

He didn't tell me
he had booked you
with the same package deal.

Fakir   or matchmaker which?

If he knew
does the whole town know?

Does it show that much?

THE BRAGGADOCIO

He asked a routine question
from his routine face
ordering me to listen
to his brags.
I spat the ground
at his feet
and walked away.

SIGN OUT TIME: NOON

I went by your hotel
an hour ago.
Looked up at Room 702
and whispered, "Hello Darling."
Of course you did not answer
"you signed out at noon,"
the clerk said.

I hated the way
she looked at me.
A teenager what would she know
about September loves.

I walked on
God only knows how far
did dumb things
like chewing clover blossoms
and de-petalling dandelion blooms.

Yesterday you said, "Don't cry dear
be happy."

"Are you?"

I smiled at passersby
but wept inside
the vacuum had to be filled
with something   why not tears?

Oh God, I'm lonely.

PATIENT'S DIAGNOSIS: ALCOHOLIC

I went to see you last night
took you the evening paper
and some poetry to read.
The smell of formaldehyde
burned my nostrils   and
the abrasive sound of starched white
bristled the air
and when I almost retched
she barked, ''What did you expect
a Hyatt Regency? This is a dryout's asylum!''
She ordered me away snapping something
about rules and hours for visitation.
At the elevator I glanced
at the waiting room with its disarray
of derelicts and disco music
a real coin-flipper for a flophouse.

Breathing fresh air again
I walked in rain
shielded myself with the newspaper
and recited poetry to the wind.

THE FINAL GOODBYE

You put me into the cab
and stood on the curb
smiling at me   with lipstick
on your lips.
My eyes spilled tears
and I could not remember
the address when the cabbie
asked me, ''Where to Miss?''
Our eyes were locked
in sadness of goodbye
until he turned the corner.
I do not know where you went
nor will I ever know
for it was the final farewell.
I only know that never can I
forget you   your touch
nor your tenderness   your kisses
or the wonderful words of love
intoned with sighs
of what we both wanted
but cannot have   a life together.
Life threw us a curve
but if we had not parted
it would have entangled us
in irreparable sorrow.
The years must dull the ache
for I cannot
live with this hurt.

SPECIAL DELIVERY

Writing a letter
to someone you love
is an art.
To say enough
but not too much
to subtly stir
but not shatter him.
Penning certain phrases
that form a pendant
hanging on the page
creating a word-picture
so that when he thinks
of you   a smile
will flit over
his face.

IT WILL NOT BE THE SAME

Every line of you
is stored in the memory bank
of my mind.
Your gentle eyes
that speak of love
louder than a screaming siren
at midnight.
Your greying temples
and curved mouth
that kiss and breathe
bliss into my body.
Oh, more is stored
the computer is full of data.
No. It will not be the same
it never can be for you
are gone.
Like an elevator sliding down
one hundred floors
my heart sank at your going
and I cannot find the key
for instant recall.

TURN OFF THE DARKNESS

The cellophane rain
    falls on the neon city
    fusing skulking shadows
    to the falsefronted buildings
    and drenches the night people
    drinking the dregs of day.

The astral haze
    darkens the mind
    to the nothingness of oblivion
    and I am speared to the apex of distress
    for I cannot find you in the chromatic lights
    of this particular night.

In my need
    to discover you
    I am lasered to an invincible wall
    indestructible in its triumph
    I wrap the darkness around me
    and slowly die within myself.

AFTERMATH

This morning wakes me
to a dark loneliness.
The scent of you
lingers in the room
and your shadow moves across
the retina again and again.
In the silence
I hear your breathing
and feel the warmth
of your flesh touching mine
and I cry inside.
The tangled threads
still weave a world
of neverness
and I wilt
like the frosted leaves
touching my feet
where we stood
not wanting to say ''goodbye''
and I watched you walk away.

BIOGRAPHICALLY SPEAKING

He does not know
my age.
He didn't ask
I didn't tell.
I know his.
I wheedled it from him
without his knowing.
He's a Sagittarian, too.

SEPARATION IS NEVER A SIMPLE THING

Winter is frosting now
and I have kept silent too long.
No. I will not forget your touch
and days delirious with color
        nor fragrance of summerscent
        nor nightscapes and inebriate dreams.

Separation is never a simple thing
for a thousand scenes appear
on the screen of despair.

I am not ready to accept the truth
        "there is no place for us."
Days drain away   their hours unshared,
and I wonder
do you
        even as I
                hurt with waiting?

I did not close the door. The click
was your quick departure.

In the cold and fragile moments
I shudder with surprise
        "you did not return."

Soon you will tire of diorama
and sense the echoing absence,
while I view scenarios
        of another season,
                and wake in the night
                        calling your name.

IT IS LIKE THAT SINCE YOU LEFT

Shall I bare
my chest
and show you
the bullet holes
or the slashes
where the blades
went through?
It is like that
since you left
so abruptly
without even a goodbye
or "I'll see you around."
Are you one of those
who gets his highs
on someone else's misery
or couldn't you face me
too shy to tell me why?

I'll give you the benefit
of the doubt.
Time will tell.

EASIER SAID BY MAIL

You dropped
the words on the page
as easily
as doing situps
before going to bed.
Sealed the envelope and
turned off love when you
licked the stamp
and flicked it in
the corner mailbox.

I recognized
your handwriting and
quickly tore it open
expecting it to drip
with love language.

Mixed with my tears
the ink ran in every direction
turning it to abstract.

I melted
to nothingness.

AFTER THE LONG SILENCE

When I heard your voice
after the long silence
it was like sharps and flats
played at the same time
like cymbals struck
on an off-beat   causing
a collision in my ears.

My head bonged with excitement.

The memories of
short encounters
came sliding down
every membrane.

With the little bit
of breath left
I, stupidly, said,
"Hi there   is that you?"

ESTRANGEMENT

It is not enough to know
we walk in the same rain,
breathe the same air
of the same city,
yet live apart.
We are not strangers
but if we passed
on the avenue
would we speak?
I have heard your footfall
on my stairs
and heard them slowly retreat.
I have passed your house,
stopped   wept   and walked away.

I fumble two dimes
in my fingers
shall I dial your number?

God, no! I am afraid
you would answer.

THE FINALITY OF GOODBYE

In the index
of my consciousness
you are listed under treasures.
Your name is at the top.
Bittersweet the parting
scourging the missing
for I don't know how to live
without you.
I touch the tomb
of dead hopes
wherein I caught
a shaft of our final sunset
and sealed in a star
that fell when I looked
to the darkening horizon
where your plane plowed
through the clouds
taking you from me.

SLOW MOTION TOUCH

Did I make too much
of the moment
when we touched
when every nerve
in your body
cried out for me.
Was I special
or have others throbbed
your groin and heart
with tom-tom beats?
Don't tell me
I do not want to know.
I want to remember
your breath on my breath
the knife-sharp pains of tension
and hear the bells
in my head bloating
my brains into submission
feel the adrenalin pouring
into my system
liquefying me with your
slow-motion touch.

WHAT WILL BE   WILL BE

Is it possible
that someday
we will look
like that gnarled
tree trunk   muscled
and anatomically lined
with distended arteries
and veins?

Will our bodies twist
and lose conformity?

We are beautifully made
convexed to the core
and molded flesh and bone.

I shall remember you as Adonis.

How will you remember me?

THE MORNING MAIL

Your package
came this morning
wrapped in brown paper
shaped like a framed picture.
I dropped it in my desk drawer
afraid of its contents
afraid it would image me
and it would be over.

    Damn you for doing this
    why didn't you toss it
    in the trash bin
    I would never have known.

I slammed the door and left
to lick my wounds.
    At the corner Drug Store
    I drank a coke   stroked
    my pride   then went back.
I opened the drawer
and angrily tore at the wrappings
and wept
my tears   wet your face.

NIGHT CALL

Like reading Braille
your fingers trace
the touch-me-nots
of my flesh
and I permit you
to do lascivious
things   but why?
I never did before.

What is that ringing
disturbing the ecstacy
of this moment?

I pick up the receiver
and it is you
calling from Phoenix.

PAGES FROM LOST YESTERDAYS

Life without you
is *not*
It sits there
on the shelf
in volumes of verse
in stereophonic sounds
and lyrics
that shake the soul.
The computered mind
does an illogic film
of past encounters now
a pointless rerun.

I turn the pages
of *lost yesterdays*
and temper the time
with remembrance.

Looking to the far horizon
searing tears mar the mirage
you stand with *arms arced*
for my coming
I do not go
for you are *not there*.

YOUR ADVICE DOESN'T WORK

I try to laugh
as you suggested
but the sound slides
downhill   back into
my throat.

POST OBITUM

I am lonesome
for you tonight
here in our house
in our room
in our bed.
I miss your tracing fingers
your breath upon my neck
the touch of love
and nuzzling closeness.
The bed is so wide now
the covers hardly ruffled.
I hug your pillow
to silence my sobbing.
Why did you go
and leave me here alone?

POST MORTEM

In the back pocket
of my mind
the lead foot of night
kicks my heart.

SOMETHING I AM NOT

If I could edit my life
to fit your journal
of what you want me to be
I would be a stereotyped being
of something I am not.

You want no imperfections
but I am only clay
with varied molds.

Sometimes I am Lorelei
singing a siren song
or seduction swathed in illusion.

Sometimes my gypsy heart
leaps when violins cry
and the moon is mellow yellow.

My roots are vagrants
running to secret places
and flamenco music
spellbinds me to rhythmic dance.

But I sit poised
and smiling at you
in the flickering candlelight.

MR. OSTENTATIOUS

In a morning-person voice
he greeted me   too probing
with that, "I know everything
about you" look.
I felt like retching.
How I wished he would vanish
like the street issue
of the Gazette
left unfolded at my doorstep
on a windy day.

SLIM TAPERS

My heart is
    an open place
        where you may come
            at any hour.

Slim tapers burn
    against strange darkness
        waiting
            for your smile.

Clutching at emptiness
    without
        inviting inward
            throbbing hurt.

Do you hear
    the drum's low beat
        when I have wars
            to win?

Occupying worlds
    we dare not leave
        lonely together
            yet so separate.

IT HAS ALL BEEN SAID BEFORE

Talking prepackaged talk
not knowing what to say
words spill from our mouths
about weather   inflation
and energy shortages.
Why don't we say
what we feel.
I know we need each other
but the timing is not right.

WRONG TIME OF DAY

The irony strikes
at night
when I am alone
after my bath
and the ten o'clock news.
I lie awake
staring at the shadows
on the ceiling
chiding myself
for sending you away
without touching you
or saying "goodbye."

FAUX PAS

I burst my cocoon
and tripped over fantasies
of phantom love
that lasted for one
short span of time.
Greedily, I plucked
the pods of passion
and tasted Mediterranean bliss.
With crushed wings
unable to fly
I drag my truncated soul
to the graveyard
of broken hearts.

COMING IN FOR THE LANDING

Fasten your seatbelt
on the way down
from a relationship.
The plunge is quick
the landing a jolt
and there is no one
at the airport
to greet you.

VISIBILITY: ZERO

I write poems
and stick them
to the refrigerator
and toss them as small change
on your dresser.
You do not read them   instead
you crumple and drop them
in the wastebasket
of your mind.

LOVE IS MUCH MORE

Love is more than a romp
in the sheets.
Sometimes it is unsmooth
like wobbling on sand
in high heels
unsure of balance.
Passion is like that
a slipping
nothing solid.

ANY AFTERNOON

Like a derelict
I perch on the bench
aimlessly tossing popcorn
to ducks in the algaed pond.
Your reflection keeps bobbing
to the surface.

YOU FINALIZED IT SO EASILY

Minor-key chords
come from the piano now.
fingers that tripped
over the keyboard
hit flats instead of sharps
and my voice cracks
at the wrong places.
My eyes burn
from heldback tears

You wrote me off
as casually as taking
a cold shower.

WHAT DID YOU EXPECT?

Did you expect me to
just walk away from you
after knowing the wonder
of you
how you smell   and taste.
After being touched
and not hurt
so deep inside.
The healing will be slow
the scar will remain.

MEDITERRANEAN FEVER

Mediterranean men
over-react
their blood flows hot
and Love is measured
by the square root
temperament by the ton.

FIVE ARE NOT ENOUGH

Because love is blind
I have five senses.
Yet, I find them
not enough.
I need a sixth sense

common sense.

YOU TAUGHT ME SO MUCH

God, we were beautiful
when we loved
back when there was time
to dream
to signature desire.
You looked through me
through the membrane
of my soul
and saw my private needs.
You taught me so much
how to listen
how to smell like promises and
endure the vacuum of waiting.

One thing you forgot
to teach me
how to live without you.

CONFESSION

I must confess to times of apprehension
For tears prevail in sleepless greying hours.
My soul cries out for human comprehension,
And seeks the haunts of Love's sequestered bowers.
The dawn tilts light and spectral ghosts take flight,
The sun-star solars sky with radiant flame
But I awake to day that's black as night
To curse the walls that press within their frame.
And though I fend against recurrent dreams,
I fail to walk the path with prudent view;
Each night, again, I thrash in rushing streams,
Clutching for bridges that lead me back to you.
My love for you has pierced with many darts
And absence is a game of bleeding hearts.

MENTAL DETOURS

Walking wounded
with freightload
of want
and Puritan guilt,
the cobbled stones
blister feet that keep
turning down side streets
named Need and Flesh.
Mental detours lead me
back to Stop sign
and a street
called Straight.

THE WAY IT IS AT FIFTY

Mid-life crises
end in hotel weekends
knocking rating charts
into cocked hats
brimming with
divorce suits.

PACIFIC PARADISE

The Garden of Eden
must be there
in the green-lush tropics
of Panama.
It brushes my heart
with its cinnamon-skinned
Adams and Eves
and its extravanganza
of Pacific backwaters
throwing its monsooned salt
upon the sands
fast-slipping back to the sea.

Chagris water slaked
my thirst
and I bathed in its flow.

I will return someday.

SOME OF EACH IS LOST

Tonight
the angry sea
and passive shore collide.

Some of each is lost.
Slushing sands
are swept away,
the sea spews
kelp and shells.
Tomorrow's sun
will warm the beach,
screaming gulls
dip for prey
while gentle waves
bathe the shore
where two hearts
met   and parted
yesterday.

EXPECTED CALL

Pummeled to death
by my own heartbeat
boom   boom   boom
like a battering ram.
I answered
the telephone
your voice.

UNDULENCY

The darkness inside
is a fearful walk
with uncertainty.
Like shifting sands
your love changes
and I slip.

STRANGE STORMS

Like a sabled cloud
you walk in inscrutable darkness.
Your eyes are wells
where strange storms brood.
You speak in tones
of want   and neverness.
Your barricaded heart
will not admit offered love.

I walk in shuddering terror
senses pulled taut   praying
they will not snap.

Loneliness stalks our shadows.

Though my heart's door is open
it will not intimidate your will.

FELICITY

Long have I sought you
among the stars at night.
In the sunshine at noonday
trying to unravel plight.

Fanned by your near image
drawn by a flickering flame,
sifting ashes for candid hope
scorched by bittered blame.

Embracing elusive shadows
parched from pseudo streams
aching solitude among the throng
searching in wasteland of dreams.

NO. 10 DISCREET STREET

The vines hang
like heavy rain
over our private alcove.
Not quite nightlike dark
but silent
except for ringing
in my head.

EVEN THE BUSY SIGNAL WOULD HELP

If I sound disconnected
it's because I am.
All day I called
your number
and the clicks
and ringing
has me spinning.
There's nothing
so disconcerting as:
"He doesn't answer Ms."

TOO TIRED TO HOLD THE DREAM

Once was
when we had everything
or so it seemed
even Time
plans were made and
promises pledged.
I collected your letters
as Susan B. Anthony dollars.
There was so much of life
of love   and joy
I kept a scrapbook
for my ego   for I was sure
things would never change
but they did.
I thought I was unforgettable
I knew you were.
I remember
your telephone number
your promises   our plans
but I am too tired
to hold the dream.

Now we have so little
almost nothing.

I WANTED TO BELIEVE YOU

The light bulb
stares down at the floor
where you stood telling
me all those lies.
Its glare yellowed your
uneasy face
and trembling lips.
You said, there was no other
but when I telephoned later
the "hello" was feminine.
I guess I knew it
but I wanted so much
to believe you.

SOME THINGS SHOULD BE LEFT UNSAID

You   say such emotions
are ungodly.

I say you are wrong.

He designed me thus.
The reason you did
not know me before
was because I kept
my feelings hidden
and ate myself up
inside.

BLITZED

Life is so cluttered
with your absence.
I try to unravel
the knots of your leaving
only to tangle them more.
Why did it happen
so suddenly?
I needed time
for bracing without
your embracing.

THE TREES BUD IN APRIL

Everytime I smell Sen Sens
I think of him.
A gentle man   my Dad.
Gaunt even in his overcoat.
Soft of voice
and vocal with praise
for every child-time accomplishment
such as an ''A'' in Arithmetic.

''You're just like him,''
my mother said. She didn't know
that made me feel all warm inside.

I wondered why he kissed
the top of my head
until the cough worsened
and I knew the awful truth.

One day I cried
and could not stop after
he told me ''when trees bud
in April I will be leaving.''

It happened on the twentieth
I was sixteen.

Every April I cry.

TO FRANCES

Tonight and every night
I will weep for you
for you are so far away
lost in your mental caverns.
I would come
but you would not know me
and I could not hear
your infectious laughter
or watch your nimble fingers
needling an AFGHAN.

How could I bear to see you
trapped inside the wall of you
looking at me as at a stranger.

HEAD OF THE HOUSE

My husband is the head
of our house.
He runs everything
    the vacuum sweeper
        the dishwasher
            dryer and washing machine
                the blender
                    even the lawnmower.

He makes
the important decisions.
    Will Castro trim his beard
        how much is the national debt
            will Carter go back to growing peanuts
            will Billy zip up his lip?

What do I do?
    Oh, I handle minor matters
        the checkbook
            Mastercharge
            Visa
                BankAmericard
                    American Express.....

TO WILMA

I see you yet
standing at my picture window
overlooking our small neoned city
your face a rapt study of parables
your hair still blown by Chicago winds
your eyes enveloping serrated mountains
and desert floor.
You did not see me
as you turned to the privacy
of my guest room
but I know
you picked up your pen
and recorded it all
in your journal.

THE TWINS

We picked their names
from our son's
bedtime prayer
and thrilled with their
daily performances
of ballet
and tumbling
in their fluid chamber.
Restless babies
miracle babies
never supposed to be
but they were.
They breathed
    and cried
        and died.

Your eyes stare sorrow
    your arms hang limp.

I sob inside
and clutch
    my   empty abdomen.

I THOUGHT I HEARD HIM CRYING

Why didn't we name him?
We had one picked
I guess we knew
he would be waxen
and breathless
not fulltermed born.
Even yet I feel
him stirring   and once
I thought I heard him crying
then he moved no more.
He is so unforgettable.
Would he have been an unaware Angel
or was he too gifted for Earth?

BACK GLANCING

Was it at the Village Inn
where we planned it all
the ranch house schematics
roughed out on a paper napkin
the split rail fence
to jump horses?
And the children
wasn't it four?
Two to look like you
and two just like me.
Things were so simple then
but so important.

PHARMACEUTICALLY SPEAKING

There should be a vaccine
against loving too deeply
hurting too much
crying too easily
and remembering too long.

PERSEVERANCE

Against great odds
He came
He cared
He cried
So did I.

He pushed a stuffed lamb
filled with music
in my arms.
We laughed and loved.
He left.
Every night I wind the lamb
lay it on my pillow
pull his love over me
and sleep.

MORNING

> Your glance goes
> right through the yellow
> caution light
> and the sign turns red   danger.
> Why can't I close my eyes
> and see green.

NOON

> You keep me dangling
> like a hang glider
> dangerously floating
> near the precipice.

NIGHT

> Everytime I wear Arpege
> I think of him
> and remember his touch.
> "You smell so good," he'd say
> and I leaned into him.
> He loved the softness.
> Every night I wear it to bed
> it's so comforting remembering.

WHY PICK ON ME?

Sardonically
Cupid grins at me
his darts still hanging
from my chest.
Why did he pick me
to bleed before the world.
What demon designated him
to drag my soul through blood
and hang me to
a Barabbas cross.

HOW COULD YOU?

You smeared your pain
upon me like an angry artist
splashing his canvas
in abstract.
You left me wounded
and gory with guilt.
You knew I was vulnerable.

MIRROR IMAGE

Like a soap opera
filling my family room
you exploit my emotions
knowing my gullibility
And like a budding teenager
I fall for the script.
The stereo plays
"Where are the clowns
send in the clowns."
I stare at myself
in the bathroom mirror.

HE IS THE ONE

Yes. He is the handsome man
with curly hair
brown going gray
so much like the tintype
of my father
soft curly hair
brown going gray.

UPON LEAVING TOCUMEN AIRPORT

The pain is deep
inside of me
flying in the azure
of your Panamanian sky.
Leaving behind love
and the beauty
of your land.
The touch of your lips
still moist on mine
and your eyes
lock my iris
blinding me to others
about me.
The tomorrows
will bring me back
to you
in memories
too wonderful ever to forget
and in the loneliness
of night
your arms will gently encircle me
and I will sleep
with your love
as my pillow.

Sonnet (Shakespearean)

NIGHTSCAPE

Tonight stark shadows fall across my bed.
The yellow sabered moon is riding high
And I become a sobbing oread,
And like a jungled beast I restless lie
Nightlong with jagged nerves and pulsing need
For unlike Eve, I cannot shake the tree
And eat the fruit unbidden. Yet indeed
I taste each morsel. My epiphany
is manifest. In moods of reverie
I wander back in search of former quest
An hour conceived to catch your fervency;
To feel the trumping throb within your breast.
The streaking dawn denies me your fierce flame,
Quixotic mortal branded with your name.

READ THE LABELS

Perhaps I made
too much of it.
I am like that
always reading labels
to make sure of contents.
He did not like
the close inspection
but as I said,
I am like that.
I had to be sure.

INTERLUDE

In the brown of Autumn
I walk through dry leaves
remembering the green summer
and you.
Going backward in dreams
backward in hope
now brittle as the twigs
under my feet

A garden squirrel
scampers up the oak
licks his paws and chatters
as if he knows my plight.
He is prepared for the cold winter
but I stand like a frosted elm
in icy neverness
crying your name
to the wind

AFTERTHOUGHTS

i

My attache case
holds the evening Gazette
a lipstick
taxi fare
and poems for you.

ii

After you left
I threw myself on the bed
trembled and sobbed.
What else could I do?
I lost you to her.

iii

Now that it is over
I walk in and out of doors
going nowhere important
no appointments to keep
no deadlines to meet
only this hangup
where to dispose dead dreams
and a ton of unwanted love.